SUPER SPIDERS

TRAPDOOR SPIDERS

BY LISA J. AMSTUTZ

PEBBLE
a capstone imprint

Published by Pebble, an imprint of Capstone
1710 Roe Crest Drive, North Mankato, Minnesota 56003
www.capstonepub.com

Library of Congress Cataloging-in-Publication Data is available on the Library of Congress website.
ISBN: 9798875224904 (hardcover)
ISBN: 9798875224539 (paperback)
ISBN: 9798875224867 (ebook PDF)

Summary: An introduction to trapdoor spiders, including where they live, what their bodies look like, how they hunt their prey, and more.

Editorial Credits
Editor: Ashley Kuehl; Designer: Bobbie Nuytten; Media Researcher: Svetlana Zhurkin; Production Specialist: Whitney Schaefer

Image Credits
Capstone: Kay Fraser (spiderweb), cover and throughout; Newscom: imageBROKER/Emanuele Biggi, 18; Science Source: A. Cosmos Blank, 13, Dr. Paul A. Zahl, 17, Francesco Tomasinelli, 19, James H. Robinson, 15; Shutterstock: All Write studio (spiderweb), 4, 8, 16, Dipak Kurmar Roy, 16, Federico.Crovetto, 10, Ken Griffiths, 4, Matteo photos, 7, Pichit Sansupa (spider), cover, back cover, 1, Pong Wira, 5, 9, 12, zaidi razak, 11, zstock, 6; Svetlana Zhurkin: 20

Printed and bound in China. PO 6274

TABLE OF CONTENTS

Hidden Homes 4

Setting a Trap 8

Handy Holes 16

Make a Spider Burrow 20

Spider Jokes 21

Glossary 22

Read More 23

Internet Sites 23

Index 24

About the Author 24

Words in **bold** are in the glossary.

HIDDEN HOMES

Trapdoor spiders are good builders. They make cozy **burrows** to live in. They even build doors! But the doors are hard to spot. They blend in with the ground.

Trapdoor spiders spin webs. The webs are thin lines outside the burrow. The spider hides inside. An insect walks by. It steps on the web. The spider feels movement. It jumps out and grabs its **prey**.

These spiders live on most **continents**. They live in warm, wet places. They make holes in dirt or near rivers.

Trapdoor spiders may be black or brown. They have eight thick legs. They have eight eyes too. Like all spiders, they have two body parts. These spiders have strong jaws. Their bite can hurt! But it will not kill you.

SETTING A TRAP

A young spider looks for a home. It finds a good spot! The spider starts to dig. Its jaws have tiny rakes that loosen the **soil**. They form it into a ball. Toss! The spider's hind legs push the dirt out of the hole.

The spider works hard. At last, the hole is ready. The spider mixes **saliva** and dirt. It coats the walls of the hole. Then it spins a **silk** web to line it.

Next, the spider makes a door for its hole. It may plug the hole like a cork. Or it may be a sheet of silk and dirt. Silk hinges hold the door in place.

The spider puts some dirt and twigs around the door. Now it is hard to see.

The spider crawls inside. It holds the door shut with its jaws. It waits and waits. Then it waits some more. Who will stumble into the trap?

Trapdoor spiders eat insects. They eat other small animals too. A frog, fish, or mouse makes a good meal.

The spider feels something move. Here comes a bug!

Zip! The spider pops out of the hole. It grabs the bug with its big **fangs**. It pulls the bug into the hole. The spider's **venom** kills the bug. Its insides turn to liquid. The spider sucks it out.

HANDY HOLES

The world is a scary place for the spider. Birds and other **predators** lurk outside. A spider would make a good snack.

The spider hides in its burrow. It holds the door shut with its jaws. Its legs push against the walls. The spider's hole helps keep it safe.

The hole is good for something else too. It is a safe place for a female to lay eggs. The spider finds a mate. Then she lays eggs in a silk sac. She keeps it safe.

Before long, the eggs hatch. The young spiders stay with their mother for months. Then they move out. It is time to make homes of their own!

MAKE A SPIDER BURROW

What You Need:

- modeling clay or Play-Doh
- plastic spider
- scissors
- cardboard
- art supplies

What You Do:

1. Make an indent in a piece of clay with your finger. This is your burrow. Place the spider inside.
2. Now build a trapdoor. Use scissors to cut a piece of cardboard to cover the burrow.
3. Decorate the door however you like.
4. Cover the burrow with the door.

SPIDER JOKES

How do spiders listen to music?

Spot-a-fly!

What's a spider's favorite place to dine out?

The all-you-can-eat bug-fet.

Why do spiders spin webs?

Because they can't knit!

What did the spider do when he got a new car?

Took it out for a spin!

GLOSSARY

burrow (BUR-oh)—a hole in the ground made or used by an animal

continent (KAHN-tuh-nuhnt)—one of Earth's seven large land masses

fang (FANG)—the biting part of a spider's mouth

predator (PRED-uh-tur)—an animal that hunts other animals for food

prey (PRAY)—an animal hunted by another animal for food

saliva (suh-LYE-vuh)—the clear liquid in the mouth

silk (SILK)—long, thin threads made by a spider

soil (SOIL)—the top layer of dirt on the ground

venom (VEN-uhm)—a poisonous liquid produced by some animals

READ MORE

Becker, Becca. *Trapdoor Spiders*. Minneapolis: Jump!, Inc., 2025.

Owen, Ruth. *Spiders: We're Not Scary—We're Amazing!* Kent, UK: Ruby Tuesday Books, 2023.

Pettiford, Rebecca. *Spiders*. Minneapolis: Bellwether Media, 2025.

INTERNET SITES

Australian Museum: Trapdoor Spiders
australian.museum/learn/animals/spiders/trapdoor-spiders-group/

Backyard Buddies: Trapdoor Spiders
backyardbuddies.org.au/backyard-buddies/trapdoor-spiders/

Britannica Kids: Trapdoor Spider
kids.britannica.com/students/article/trapdoor-spider/313879

INDEX

burrows, 4, 5, 17

digging, 8

doors, 4, 10, 11, 12, 17

eggs, 18, 19

eyes, 7

fangs, 14

jaws, 7, 8, 12, 17

legs, 7, 8, 17

predators, 16

prey, 5

silk, 8, 10, 18

venom, 14

ABOUT THE AUTHOR

Lisa Amstutz is the author of more than 150 children's books on topics ranging from applesauce to zebra mussels. An ecologist by training, she enjoys sharing her love of nature with kids. Lisa lives on a small farm with her family.